The Abyss

Poems for Our World

by

Geza Tatrallyay

Deux Voiliers Publishing

2022

The Abyss: Poems for Our World

First Edition 2022

Copyright © Geza Tatrallyay

All Rights Reserved

ISBN 978-1-928049-57-9

Published in Canada by

Deux Voiliers Publishing, Aylmer, Quebec.

www.deuxvoilierspublishing.com

Editor - Ian Thomas Shaw

Cover Design – Ian Thomas Shaw

Cover Photo – Ian Thomas Shaw

For my granddaughter, Lara

Acknowledgements

Questions for us, My poems grow like a tree, What color was coral, Homo postcoronavirus and *The nightmare of nihil* were published in **Terror House Magazine** in April 2021

Lay Down Your Arms, Brother was posted in store windows in **Poem Town**, Randolph VT during Poetry Month, April 2021 and included in their annual anthology

Haiku: the wail of the wind was posted in store windows in **Poem City**, Montpelier VT during Poetry Month, April 2021

My poems *Homo postcoronavirus* and *Let's ring in the New Year* were posted in store windows in **Poem Town**, St. Johnsbury VT during Poetry Month, April 2021

Send an SOS out into space was published in **Bloodroot Literary Magazine**, Vol. 13, 2021

My poems *Homo postcoronavirus, COVID Verses* and *Christmas Eve twenty-twenty* have been included in the **Vermont History COVID Archive**

My sincerest thanks go to Ian Shaw of Deux Voiliers Publishing for agreeing to publish this little volume (along with the two others in different genres DVP has already published), to my agent, Lucinda Clark, for her support and guidance throughout my career since 2015 when she brought my first poetry collection, *Cello's Tears* into the world, to Megha Sood, for her generous comments in the Foreword and to all the readers of, and listeners to, my poetry and other works.

Table of Contents

Foreword   01

Introduction   07

I. The beautiful world ...

My friend, the crescent moon   09
Spring wakes up one morning   10
The spider's web   11
A black, ringed snake   12
The dead phoebe   13
Looming thunderstorm   14
Our lilacs are blooming   15
The foghorn   16
Haiku: the pond beckons me   17
Haiku: stardust from heaven   18
Haiku: Milky Way   19
Haiku: wet snow   20
Haiku: the wail of the wind   21
Haiku: another sunset   22
Haiku: Angry clouds   23
Haiku: no stars   24

II. Our pleasures ...

The dying fire	25
When I lie there in our communal bed ...	26
You are no longer here with me	27
Perfected rapture	28
Photographs are all I have	29
Purple petunia	30
The essence of your touch	31
Still lusting	32
Haiku: scented pines	33
Haiku: scallops and garlic	34
Haiku: blueberry pancakes	35
Haiku: baking bread	36
Haiku: Snow in October	37
Haiku: Moon Glow	38
Haiku: lingering tastes	39
The wakeful mind	40
My poems grow like a tree	41
Sitting on the throne	42
A good friend is no more ...	43
Haiku: the spinning mind	44
Haiku: wine, women and weed	45
Three haiku for my grandson, Sebastian	46
A good friend is no more ...	47

III. And how we destroy it all …

The Abyss	48
Questions for us	49
The climate is changing	50
Swirls of plastic swim in the seas	51
A deathly silence reigns out there	52
Snowflakes dance a wild flamenco	53
Satanic wolves	54
What color was coral	55
The universe and mankind	56
Haiku: a whale kills a man	57
My little Lara	58
This is not a happy country	59
Fake rhetoric	60
Haiku: trumpeting	61
Words can kill too …	62
We find reasons to kill …	63
What can we give thanks for	64
I weep with the rain …	65
Haiku: the sun burns the fog	66
Haiku: war brings screaming bombs	67

IV. I plead for humanity …

Send an SOS out into space	68
Haiku: we are all humans	69

Haiku: black, brown, white, yellow	70
Lay down your arms brother	71
America, give up your guns	72
We are the masked great ape …	73
Christmas Eve twenty-twenty	74
Let's ring in the New Year …	75
COVID verses	76
Homo postcoronavirus	78
Alas, our world is no longer	79
Afterlife	80
The nightmare of nihil	81
About the Author	83
Other Books by Geza Tatrallyay	85
Also from Deux Voiliers Publishing	87

Foreword

Geza Tatrallyay has taken up the mantle of telling truth in various genres. As a Rhodes Scholar in Human Sciences, a graduate in human ecology from Harvard University, and someone who has worked in close quarters with clean energy sectors, Geza has passionately used his experience to discuss various social and environmental issues plaguing our times like human trafficking, immigration and displacement issues, and global warming in all his previous collections of poetry, memoirs, novels, and short stories.

In his riveting fifth collection of poetry, this prolific poet and author passionately urges humankind to take stock of its senseless actions leading to the imbalance in nature causing devastating and irreversible changes to our climate. The collection sits at the inter-section of natural beauty and its destruction caused by humankind. *The Abyss: Poems for Our World* serves as a clarion call to change our ways and to work towards the restoration of a world that we are hell-bent on destroying.

This brilliant volume is divided into four parts namely *"The beautiful world ...," "Our pleasures ...," "And how we destroy it all ...,"* and *"I plead for humanity ..."* In his fifteenth book, Geza talks passionately about how human beings sitting at the top of the social chain are a prominent threat to nature. Through various poems in his collection, he points toward the failure of humankind to come to an agreement to protect mother earth. The current pandemic is a testament to the fact that senseless actions are leading to the systematic destruction of our beautiful world and everything in it.

In the first part, *"The beautiful world ...,"* Geza talks about the natural beauty we are bestowed with and its endless bounty. How the world around us is a constant source of inspiration for our creative ways. Through vivid imagery and visceral language, the poet urges readers to respect and protect the environment that nourishes all living beings let alone us humans. Through his poems, he poignantly points out how utterly senseless acts by human beings have caused an imbalance in nature. The frail balance that is so difficult to maintain let alone restore.

The profundity of myriad human emotions is deftly balanced with the poet's masterful play of words. Through various haiku in this book, Geza succinctly captures the beauty and profoundness of mother nature. He points us towards important learning that in nature everything competes for its share yet maintains a delicate and necessary balance.

In the second part of the collection, *"Our pleasures ...,"* the poet ingeniously explores the brilliance of human emotions and pleasures we derive from the natural world around us. Through his poem *"My poems grow like a tree"* and several haiku, Geza brilliantly paints a view of his creative process for readers. The poet also talks about how our creative expressions transcend our identity beyond death. In the poem *"The sameness of being,"* he points toward the triviality of human life in a deep introspective manner.

The second part is a beautiful exegesis of our world suffused with the beauty of music, food, natural elements, and human emotions. The poet also brilliantly delves into the discussion of loss and pain as integral emotions along with the deep exploration of love which is deeply infused in all of us.

In the third part of the book, *"And how we destroy it all ..."*, the poet fiercely draws attention to the urgency of climate change, global warming, and other atrocities our world is actively facing. Geza points toward various disasters such as intense heat, rising sea levels, and drought causing long-term shifts in temperature and weather patterns. Through his poems, he feverishly declares how human activities have been the main source of climate change causing irreversible and dangerous impact on our world. How we are heading towards our own extinction through these mindless acts.

Geza through lyrical activism draws attention to various ill effects of climate change such as coral bleaching and destruction of reefs caused by rising temperature of seas and melting polar caps. In his poems *"The Universe and Mankind," "I weep with the rain"* and *"What can we give thanks for,"* he exposes the incessant greed of humankind and its senseless actions that are slowly leading us toward the cataclysmic extinction of our beautiful planet.

As a literary activist and poet, I'm drawn to the poems *"This is not a happy country"* and *"Fake rhetoric,"* where Geza pulls our attention to the despondent state of social-political justice in our country that leads to the suppression of underrepresented communities and people of color. He also alerts us to the subtle fact that history repeats itself and through misinformation and failure to act we never learn the lesson it teaches.

Geza as a poet informs us how words hold the power to spread misinformation and can cause equal damage as loaded weapons. The poet talks about the hopelessness of the human mind amid climate change, wars, pandemics, and riots ravaging the nation and the world.

Geza covers the quintessential topic of increasing gun violence in the country and the nation's incessant greed for guns. The end of the collection also deeply focuses on the ravaging impact of the pandemic and its deep effect on our social life. The ill-effects of the pandemic along with its depressing effects of isolation are deeply explored in his poems. Geza's book comes full circle at the tail end of the collection *"I plead for humanity ...,"* where through his passionate and skillful play of words he pleads to humanity to take stock of its greed-filled actions and to work towards a sustainable future. A responsibility that we are bestowed with.

The entire collection, *"The Abyss,"* calls us to work towards building a better and loving world. Through deft poetic brilliance coupled with the sensitivity of an activist poet, Geza Tatrallyay is feverishly urging humans to be aware of the senseless destruction they are causing to the world while threatening the survival of their fellow beings thus creating an imbalance.

This stunning collection not only explores the beauty of the natural world and the pleasures we derive from it but also discusses the harrowing effects of human-induced climate change while passionately urging its readers to work towards the shared responsibility of sustaining it. I'm immensely thankful to Geza Tatrallyay for bringing this thoughtful collection to its readers.

Megha Sood
New Jersey

Introduction

This collection, my fifth collection of poetry and my fifteenth book, poignantly sets out that we – human beings – are the greatest threat to life and this world: not only because of our social and political divisions, but also because of our continuing incapacity to come to terms with the need to change our ways, and to adopt behaviors that are less destructive to mother earth, other species of life and indeed, ourselves. The current pandemic we are living, is, in many ways, an example of how these factors interact.

My last two collections of poetry, *Extinction* and *Extinction Rebellion*, were devoted to exploring the beauty of nature around us and more specifically, how our actions are systematically destroying it. *The Abyss* continues the focus on our glorious world and the delight we can derive from it and from each other, as well as on the manner in which our habits can have such a harmful impact.

I sincerely hope that my readers will see these poems as a call to action for us to live our lives differently—certainly with more respect for each other, ourselves and the world around us!

Geza Tatrallyay
Barnard, Vermont

I. The beautiful world …

My friend, the crescent moon

My friend, the crescent moon,
a sliver of silver,
in the twilight heavens,
the lighthouse in the sky
that guides and comforts me
through this threatening night
enveloping the world—

when will day come again?

Spring wakes up one morning

Spring wakes up one morning
and the world is renewed:
the sun smiles on us as
winter's snow and ice melt,
and earth molts its white coat,
a snake shedding its skin,
trees dress in bright colors
for the summer season,
creeks gush with melt water
and nourishing rains pour,
turning brown grass verdant,
pink and yellow buds appear
and blossom into leaves
or multi-hued flowers,
fiddleheads poke their pates
above the dark topsoil,
unseen peepers chirrup
in transient vernal pools
where ducks land to find food,
robins nest in the eaves
and lay their blue-green eggs—
spring wakes up one morning
and the world is renewed.

The spider's web

A spider spins a spool of spit,
that ever so fine filament,
into a tough, filigree web—
a death trap for wayfaring flies
and other flying bugs and beasts
that it will munch on with delight.

Only the arachnid can scoot
with its long legs along those threads
to get at its perishing prey.

Do not destroy its perfect mesh,
this delicate but sturdy snare
that both destroys and sustains life.

A black, ringed snake

Down by our pond I lifted a flat rock:
a squirming, slithering snake startled me,
bedecked in its scaly, grey-black armor,
bright orange neck ring and underbelly—
the serpent's forked tongue darted in and out,
as if wanting to say, "This is my space!"

Frightened, at first I recoiled, then stood back
and admired my reptile friend's perfection
as it slid in silence into a hole,
escaping this hominid intruder—

Just for a brief moment, I wondered at
our rather predictable responses,
both my human and the reptilian—
survival, programmed by evolution.

The dead phoebe

I found a phoebe on the porch—
she lay there, dead, I know not why.

I wondered: did she have children,
how many eggs has she hatched,
how many have flown from her nest,
will the bird be missed by anyone
but me, who heard her call her name,
fee-bee, fee-bee, when I approached?

Now that my phoebe is no more,
will anyone miss me when I die?

Looming Thunderstorm

The summer air hangs heavy:
nighttime consolidates.

Billowing cloud cover
hides the moon and the stars.

A looming thunderstorm
shudders, ready to burst
with the pointillist throb
of cathartic rainfall
and blanket Mother Earth
in the sky's orgasmic
and comforting release.

It will soon be over.

Our lilacs are blooming

Our lilacs are blooming,
lavender, pink and white:
their heady fragrance,
sweet, intoxicating,
bewitches my nostrils.
Swallowtail butterflies
flutter from leaf to leaf,
yellow, orange and black,
adding color to the
sensual ecstasy;
a hummingbird hovers
pecking at each flower
to suck up the nectar,
bumblebees, too, buzz
as they flit in and out
competing for their share,
nature's magnificence,
there, alive in one bush!

The Foghorn

with its low belly-aching bleats
the foghorn warns passing vessels
of rocks and maritime traffic—

ominous and otherworldly,
its welcome droning reassures:
someone is watching out for us

on these murky, gloomy stretches
that we must boldly navigate,
risking it all to get through life

a false sense of security,
though a comforting easy sound
that takes the fear from the passage

Haiku: the pond beckons me

the pond beckons me:
crayfish nibble on my toes
my friends, the frogs, croak

Haiku: stardust from heaven

Lighting my way home,
fireflies float among the trees—
stardust from heaven

Haiku: Milky Way

Along the night sky
I follow the Milky Way
through the universe

Haiku: wet snow

The program read rain
but blobs of wet snow dance—
nature changed its mind

Haiku: the wail of the wind

The wail of the wind
wafting through wintry trees—
a woodwind's weeping

Haiku: another sunset

another sunset
blazes across the heavens
lighting up my soul

Haiku: Angry Clouds

Angry clouds tango
to the music of the frogs,
those thundering gods

Haiku: no stars

No stars, cloudy night,
a loon's tremolo portends,
calamity looms

II. Our pleasures ...

The dying fire

The faint flame from the dying fire
flickers just enough with the breeze
to light up your eyes in the night—
they tell me that you still love me,
a glance that reassures, comforts.

The hint of a beguiling smile,
a whiff of your floral fragrance,
here, snuggling next to my body,
fill my heart with such happiness—
the fire dies, but our love does not.

When I lie there in our communal bed ...

When I lie there in our communal bed,
unconscious, seemingly already dead,
dear, just whisper I love you in my ear
and kiss me one last time, like you used to,
and I will be happy forevermore.

You are no longer here with me

One fleeting moment to the next,
you are no longer here with me:
although some cells in your body
may still stay alive for a while
after your heart stops pumping blood
to the brain and all your organs—

But the miracle of your mind,
the loving look in your soft eyes,
the complex nexus of feeling,
of knowledge and understanding
that made you, you—the one I loved,
is no longer, gone forever—

A lifeless, unfeeling carcass,
a mass of organic matter
that slowly decomposes, rots
is what lies here before me now.

What of you remains in my mind,
what I nurture and keep alive,
that flame flickers and fades away:
with time, your memory, too, dies.

Perfected rapture

Hearing Yo Yo Ma play
the six Bach cello suites
I float toward heaven
in perfected rapture

Photographs are all I have

Photographs are all I have
to remember you, dear mother—
once we were one, I within you,
me, your egg fertilized by sperm
from my father, your husband—

I knew your body, inside out:
I exited between your thighs,
left your warmth for the cruel world,
but you held me close to your skin
and had me suckle at your breasts.

You cared for me when I was sick,
cooked for me, sang and read to me,
taught me language and manners,
sparing no time or energy
to make me a better person.

You lavished such love on your son
only a mother could or would.

Alas, you departed this world
of flesh and blood some years ago
but I look at myself and know
that we are still one being and
you will always live on in me
though my memory of you fades.

The purple petunia
(to my first granddaughter, Sophia)

You poke at the purple petunia
with those *petite* baby fingers of yours:
your smile, Sophia, your dada goo goos,
proclaiming your pleasure with this strange toy,
your eyes declare your curiosity
and wonder at its fragile perfection,
your mind soaking in the natural world
all around you with its many marvels
as each blossom adds to who you become,
a beautiful budding flower yourself

The essence of your touch

The essence of your touch
still lingers on my skin,
silken and palpable.

It is all I have left
of you I can cling to,
now that, love, you are gone.

But soon, even that dream
drifts into the darkness:
my life becomes a void.

Still lusting

A squirming sea of flesh and skin
covered with tiny beads of sweat,
of tousled hair, the odd eyeball
roving across the horizon,
an orgy of orgasmic thrills
seems to await my throbbing self—
I strip naked, and dive, lustful,
into the vortex of this dream,
then wake beside you, still lusting,
but this time only after you.

Haiku: scented pines

I walk in the woods,
lost among the scented pines
with my thoughts of you

Haiku: scallops and garlic

Scallops and garlic
linguine with white wine sauce:
my favorite meal

Haiku: blueberry pancakes

blueberry pancakes
with Vermont maple syrup:
delicious breakfast

Haiku: baking bread

My stomach perks up:
the whiff of my bread baking
wafts from the kitchen

Haiku: Snow in October

Snow in October:
icing sugar coats the land.
Your body warms mine.

Haiku: Moon glow

Moon glow on the snow
lights the path in the forest,
the way to your heart

Haiku: lingering tastes

tuna sashimi,
to drink: daiginjo sake—
the lingering tastes

The wakeful mind

The wakeful mind, at night in bed,
stresses and magnifies issues
leftover from the day's struggles,
weaves them into dreams too vivid
or those terrifying nightmares
with metamorphosed, haunting
characters from past and present,
who bring a strange resolution,
or derail the plot before death
as the mind wakes to face the light

My poems grow like a tree

My poems grow like a tree,
ideas germinate
in the mind's fertile soil:
tonal words with meaning
emerge, and like fresh shoots,
sprout into rhythmic lines.

New thoughts, new directions
spread their roots, their tendrils,
lo, a metaphor forms—
a freshly budding bough—
and an image blossoms
like a fragrant flower.

Alliterations buzz
like summer bumblebees
in my ecstatic ear—
a perfected picture
with transcendent music,
painted with few words.

Sitting on the throne

I compose this poem
while I sit on the throne,
butt bare, to piss and shit,
ousting my supposed soul—

my being most exposed,
struggling to perform
that necessary deed—

my alliterations,
my metaphors peppered
with gastral grunts and groans—

a natural poem
every creature lives.

A good friend is no more
(On learning of the death of Peter Fox Smith)

A good friend is no more.

When I read his poems though,
he comes alive again:

his voice will not die.

Haiku: the spinning mind

The inspired mind spins
a thought into a story,
or at night, a dream

Haiku: Wine, women and weed

Wine, women and weed
wrestle those worries away
as we waddle on

Three haiku for my grandson, Sebastian

My grandson Sebö
loves to win at memory:
he often beats me

My grandfather Gez
loves to lose at memory:
I always whip him

Torta di Noci
baked by my grandma Mimi:
a yummy dessert

The sameness of being

The sameness of being,
this tedium of rot,
the inescapable
senselessness of our lives,
the tragedy of death
that brings us all to nought,
our puny achievements
lost in the vast cosmos,
lives become forgotten
as human memory,
too, fades away with time.

Just live your bloody life
for those ephemeral
few moments of pleasure!

III. And how we destroy it all ...

The Abyss

We wake from our wanton lifestyle
our consumptive ways—
we poisoned the world around us,
razed our primeval forests,
now gasp for clean air to breathe,
our reservoirs are dry,
our lips parched,
rising seas wash away our towns,
no food for our children
but our automatic weapons
will kill them in their schools or homes.
We stand not knowing what to do
on the edge of the abyss,
this self-wrought *Walpurgisnacht*
of humanity's extinction,
Only want and suffering await
and then the eternal nihil.

Questions for us

Our fellow species on this earth
are magnificent, eccentric beasts,
creations of evolution
over many millennia.

Why do we not respect them more,
these other wondrous forms of life?

Why do we murder them for food,
or willy-nilly for pleasure,
burn the woods and steppes they live in,
pour chemicals and shit into
the rivers and lakes where they swim?

Why do we poison the water,
so necessary for all life,
pollute the air we and they breathe?

Why are we recklessly driving
us all to shameful extinction?

The climate is changing

The climate is changing
our ice cap is melting
sea levels are rising
there is drought everywhere
or torrential rainfall
our forests are burning
the smoke is choking us
we cannot see the moon
or stroll the Milky Way
the sun does not come up
we are dying on earth
this planet we have ruined

Swirls of plastic swim in the seas

Swirls of plastic swim in the seas
deathly fodder for fish, seabirds,
turtles, even dolphins and whales
and ultimately ourselves.

We throw out our used plastic bags
but then end up ingesting them
killing many living beings
unwittingly along the way.

Our profligate stupidity
will result in our extinction.

A deathly silence reigns out there

A deathly silence reigns out there:
birds do not sing their morning song,
eventide, crickets do not chirp,
there are no frogs left to ribbit,
no dog to bark across the road,
skeleton trees do not sport leaves
to whisk the whisper of the wind,
the heat and drought have killed all life,
corpses litter the land, ours too—
a deathly silence reigns out there.

Snowflakes dance a wild flamenco

Snowflakes dance a wild flamenco,
blustered by the raging blizzard,
hither and thither, all around—
winds howl shrieking through window cracks,
cold seeps into and through our bones
and we shiver under blankets,
freezing, and in trepidation
of the unearthly destruction
of climate change, sure to follow
and wash away this world of ours.

Satanic wolves

Satanic wolves cavort on my mother,
gnaw at her flesh, drink of her blood,
hooves prancing wildly on Gaia—

the witches' cauldron of human waste,
the debris of a warmed-up world,
empties on her ailing corpus.

Can we still save our mother earth,
or will she perish with mankind?

What color was coral

What color was coral,
now all bleached white?

Multihued it was, once,
before the oceans warmed
and turned more acidic
from all that CO2
we spew into the air,
expelling the algae
living in its polyps
in symbiotic love.

The algae turn toxic,
the coral reefs whither,
nature is diminished,
and beauty is destroyed.

We have done it again.

The universe and mankind

Neutron stars collide, creating black holes,
ripples in space-time and gamma ray bursts,
and strangely, also gold and platinum.

Some black holes gobble up galaxies,
asteroids ram into stars and planets,
bringing mass extinction where there is life.

Homo sapiens evolved here on earth:
our relentless consumptive lifestyle
now fouls our world, changing its climate
and bringing floods and storms, drought and famine.

In the end, therefore, rather perversely,
is mankind's sole role in the universe
to destroy earth, this nest that nurtured us?

The one fatal flaw in evolution?

Haiku: a whale kills a man

A whale kills a man:
how many whales have we killed
to harvest blubber?

My little Lara

My little Lara loves to loll
on her cuddly baby blanket
or to ride horsey on my knees,
snuggle with her loving parents

a wee wisp of a wondrous waif
with not a worry in her world
of love and mother's milk,
sleep and those bodily functions ...

I dread the globe she will inherit
with its eight billion people
sucking on its scarce resources
and wielding one billion guns
as they drive life forms on earth
to cataclysmic extinction

This is not a happy country

This is not a happy country,
where an uncaring few govern
to enrich themselves and their friends,
where the poor can't pay doctors' bills
and don't have enough for the rent,
nor even to feed their children,
where people of color are killed
or prevented from advancing,
where immigrants are not welcome,
institutions do not function
and politics are polarized.
This is not a happy country:
it is a failing third-world state
that does not work for its people.

So, brothers, let's rise up and fight
against this ingrained corruption
and let us all work together
to create a better future
for our children, for you and me,
for all species of life on earth.

Brothers, let us rise up and fight!

Fake rhetoric

Fake rhetoric fans the fires of fear,
stokes the smoldering embers of hatred:

*"kill before they kill you and torch your home,
loot your belongings and rape your daughter—
those protesters are scum who want to destroy
this America we made great again ..."*

or so goes the abhorrent bombast
spewed at us by the fascist populists
who maneuvered themselves to power,
and now only want to line their pockets
and those of their fawning, sycophant friends—

we are reliving Weimar Germany,
the rise of Hitler and Mussolini,
or will this be Stalin's U.S.S.R?

Haiku: trumpeting

Trump trumpets self-love
and demands adulation
but does he govern?

Words can kill too ...

Words can kill too, not just your guns.

They can give license to murder,
incite a mob to run amok.

Hateful language, like loaded guns,
will rouse the rabble to rampage
and will lead to a killing spree.

Be careful of the words you shout
from the extremist, populist
pulpit you usurp from Hitler,
Stalin, Mussolini or Trump.

People in packs are just like rats
ready to follow any sign
and turn it into violence.

We find reasons to kill ...

Why swat a fly when it flies in your face?
A mosquito that tries to bite your arm?
Why cull a crayfish that swims in your pond?
Why trap a mouse that likes to share your house?
Why shoot a fox that chews up your chickens?
Why slaughter a pig to devour its chops?
Why butcher a bull that skewers your son?
Why murder a neighbor who screws your wife?

We find reasons to kill other beings
To justify our murdering instinct
Instead of existing in peace with them.

What can we give thanks for
(Thanksgiving Day, 2020)

What can we give thanks for
when the virus rages
killing friends and loved ones,
decimating mankind

What can we give thanks for
when the climate changes
bringing on floods and fires
and we are the culprits

What can we give thanks for
when fascists gain power
destroy democracy
as we delude ourselves

What can we give thanks for
when brother kills brother
because his skin is black
racism lives on in us

What can we give thanks for
only the shared moments
the touch of a loved one
the beauty of nature

What can we give thanks for
it is all too fleeting,
we all return to dust
will our world die with us?

I weep with the rain ...

I weep with the rain for the world we used,
for the ancient forests our wildfires burned,
the grasslands we turned to searing desert,
the seas filled with plastic and overfished,
the smoggy, smoky air we now must breathe,

for my grandchildren: how will they survive?

Haiku: the sun burns the fog

The sun burns the fog
and the world appears again
till smoke smothers all

Haiku: war brings screaming bombs

War brings screaming bombs
Destruction and death
And then eternal silence

IV. I plead for humanity ...

Send an SOS out into space

Send an SOS out into space:
there might be intelligent life
out there in this vast universe.

Please, come save us, you aliens,
please save our worthwhile creations,
our Mona Lisa and Hamlet,
Bach's sublime solo cello suites,
our scant scientific knowledge—
which, no doubt, just pales beside yours.

Alien friends, have pity on us
miserable human beings,
this fallible living species
that has destroyed its planet.

Please, come save us, you aliens!

Haiku: we are all humans

We are all humans
your color does not matter
let's love each other

Haiku: black, brown, white, yellow

Black, brown, white, yellow:
we are all human beings—
why not respect me?

Lay down your arms brother

Lay down your arms brother,
come here and embrace me
(now, figuratively,
while Covid still plagues us) —

Why all this enmity?
Why you want to shoot me?
What did I do to you?

We are all made equal,
I have hands, feet like you,
eyes, nose, mouth, ears and hair—
only my skin color
is a little darker.

Do not pull the trigger;
let us work together
to make this land better,
to create a country
that welcomes all mankind.

America, give up your guns

America, give up your guns:
come on man, for fuck's sake, tell me,
why do you think you need these arms?

Three hundred fifty million
weapons to murder your neighbors,
your wife in a fit of anger,
or for your child to shoot his friend?

That's more than one for each person,
one for every man, woman, child,
and each month now you are buying
two million more such firearms,
because ... are you scared that someone else
will enter your home or space
and you need to defend yourself
or is it all just to show off—
but three Kalashnikovs, four Glocks
in your arsenal—what the hell?

The police, too, are trained to kill:
they all assume that you are armed—
if you happen to be a Black
you're guilty because of your skin.

America, give up your guns:
come on man, for fuck's sake, tell me,
why do you think you need these arms?

Why can't you love your fellow man?

We are the masked great ape ...

Our faces are covered:
we are the masked great ape,
now cowering in fear
of some nano-virus.

This pandemic panic
destroys our livelihoods,
strains our relationships,
reshapes society.

But better still alive,
still breathing and feeling,
than buried underground
in some improvised grave.

We are the masked great ape,
no longer absolute
ruler of this jungle,
the world we have ruined.

Christmas Eve twenty-twenty

Christmas Eve twenty-twenty is finally here,
I just settled my brains for a long winter's nap,
and alone I wait with great anticipation
for the joyful sound of hooves pawing on the roof,
the dancing and prancing of eight tiny reindeer.

Will our old Saint Nick come down the chimney this year
to bring the presents I asked for in my letter?

Or, instead of biting on the stump of his pipe,
is our dear, chubby and plump, right jolly old elf,
our immuno-compromised, obese Santa Claus
now sucking oxygen from a ventilator
in the ICU of some over-run hospital
somewhere near the North Pole, cared for by his elves,
all infected by the dreaded COVID virus?

Will he survive to perform his act next Christmas?

Let's ring in the New Year …
(New Year's Eve, 2020)

Let's ring in the New Year with glee
and banish this one with no tears:
it brought such pain, so many deaths
suffering and uncertainty,
poverty caused by the virus,
people left homeless by climate,
by wildfires, floods and hurricanes,
the ugly voice of extremists,
the deaths of brothers and sisters
killed by those meant to protect them,
the rich, of course, getting richer
the poor only poorer, each day—

Let's ring in the New Year with hope:
vaccines to defeat the virus,
a brand-new administration
that cares for the people it serves,
the environment they live in,
the future they and their children have,
clean air to breathe, water to drink,
and unpolluted food to eat—

Let's ring in the New Year and work,
hold hands to build a better world!

COVID Verses

I

I am livid
that my friend
has caught COVID.

Is this his end?

II

Did we get it,
Covid-19?

Let's quarantine,
wash our hands well,
keep our distance,
check for fever.

Phew, it's a cold
Do not panic.
We may not die.
No, not just yet.

III

Millions died
the world over:
like Spanish flu,
this one, too, kills,

especially
when our leaders
are greedy hacks,
who do not care
for our welfare,
just their own skin
and pocketbooks.

Homo postcoronavirus

We are all premature corpses:
death masks now cover our faces
as we walk around like zombies,
not touching, feeling or hugging
our fellow ghost-like creatures.

We quake with the frigid frisson
of fear that we might just crumble
into viral dust with the next breath.

At night we return to our tombs
of anxiety and terror,
and wake to morbid statistics.

Will there be at least one Adam
and one Eve who survive this plague
to spawn a new kind of being?

One, who will treat this world better,
not destroy its fellow species,
the land, sea and air all around,
a wiser and kinder human,
Homo postcoronavirus.

Alas, our world is no longer

Alas, our world is no longer,
our lives have changed once and for all;
devastating global warming,
this vile virus have made it so.

No more the handshake, the double kiss,
the carefree embrace of old friends,
prickly masks hide smiles and frowns now
and we dare not be with our kind.

Will we see far-away loved ones,
hold the new grandchild born elsewhere,
share a moment or two with friends,
travel again to see the world?

Love, is it just you and I now,
for the rest of our time on earth?

Afterlife

When I die, will the heat and rain decay my flesh,
or will maggots still be around to feed on me?
Will there still be trees for my body to nourish,
or will my chemicals just seep into the earth,
uselessly, like the life we live, with no purpose?

Is this the afterlife all living things die for?

The nightmare of nihil

The nightmare of nihil
that incorporeal,
non-sentient status,
where the body decays
and one barely exists
in the minds of loved ones,
and only till they die,
or perhaps as a name
engraved on a tombstone,
a row of letters,
the rich life forgotten,
all washed away by time—
that is everyone's fate
so live out this dream
hedonistically,
enjoy it while you can!

About the Author

Born in Budapest, Geza Tatrallyay escaped with his family from Communist Hungary in 1956 during the Revolution, immigrating to Canada. After attending the University of Toronto Schools and serving as School Captain in his last year, he attended Harvard College, graduating in 1972 with a B.A. in Human Ecology, and, as a Rhodes Scholar from Ontario, obtained a B.A. / M.A. in Human Sciences from Oxford University in 1974. He completed his studies with a M.Sc. from London School of Economics and Politics in 1975. Geza worked as a host in the Ontario Pavilion at Expo 70, the world's fair in Osaka, Japan, and represented Canada in epée fencing at the Montreal Olympics in 1976. His professional experience has included stints in government, international finance and environmental entrepreneurship. Geza is a citizen of Canada and Hungary, and, as a green card holder, currently divides his time between Barnard, Vermont and San Francisco. He is married to Marcia, and their daughter, Alexandra, lives in San Francisco with husband David, and two sons, Sebastian and Orlando, while their son, Nicholas, lives in Nairobi with his Hungarian wife, Fanni, and his granddaughters, Sophia and Lara. Geza is also the author of five novels, three memoirs, four poetry collections (plus, of course, this one), a short story collection and a children's picture storybook. His poems, stories, essays and articles have been published in journals in Canada and the USA.

Other Books by Geza Tatrallyay

Arctic Meltdown, (thriller) e-published on Amazon and www.smashwords.com, December 2011

Twisted Reasons, (thriller, first in 'Twisted' trilogy) November 2014, Deux Voiliers Publishing

Cello's Tears, (poetry collection) May 2015, P.R.A. Publishing

For the Children, (memoir) May 2015, Editions Dedicaces

The Expo Affair, (memoir) April 2016, Guernica Editions

Twisted Traffick, (thriller, second in 'Twisted' trilogy) October 2017, Black Opal Books

Sighs and Murmurs, (poetry collection) April 2018, P.R.A. Publishing

Twisted Fates, (thriller, third in 'Twisted' trilogy) June 2018, Black Opal Books

The Waffle and the Pancake, (children's picture storybook), September 2018, Bayeux Arts

The Rainbow Vintner, (thriller) February 2019, Black Opal Books

The Fencers, (memoir) March 2019, Deux Voiliers Publishing

Extinction, (poetry collection) April 2019, P.R.A. Publishing

Extinction Rebellion, (poetry collection) July 2020, Cyberwit

Arctic Meltdown, 2nd Updated Edition, (thriller), August 28, 2021, Black Opal Books

The Mind Spins, (short story collection), November 2021, P.R.A. Publishing

Also From
Deux Voiliers Publishing

Soldier, Lily, Peace and Pearls by Con Cú (2012)
Last of the Ninth by Stephen L. Bennett (2012)
Marching to Byzantium by Brendan Ray (2012)
Tales of Other Worlds by Chris Turner (2012)
Bidong by Paul Duong (Literary Fiction 2012)
Zaidie and Ferdele by Carol Katz (2012)
Sumer Lovin' by Nicole Chardenet (2013)
Kirk's Landing by Mike Young (2014)
Romulus by Fernand Hibbert and translated by Matthew Robertshaw (2014)
Palawan Story by Caroline Vu (2014)
Cycling to Asylum by Su J. Sokol (2014)
Stage Business by Gerry Fostaty (2014)
Stark Nakid by Sean McGinnis (2014)
Twisted Reasons by Geza Tatrallyay (2014)
Four Stones by Norman Hall (2015)
Nothing to Hide by Nick Simon (2015)
Frack Off by Jason Lawson (2015)
Wall of Dust by Timothy Niedermann (2015)
The Goal by Andrew Caddell (2015)
Quite Perfectly Dead by Geri Newell Gillen (2016)
Return to Kirk's Landing by Mike Young (2016)
This Country of Mine by Didier Leclair and translated by Elaine Kennedy (2018)

Pretenders by Fernand Hibbert and translated by
Matthew Robertshaw (2018)
The Fencers by Geza Tatrallyay (2019)I
The Marginal Ride Anthology edited by Ian Thomas
Shaw and Timothy Niedermann (2019)

www.deuxvoilierspublishing.com

www.ingramcontent.com/pod-product-compliance
Lightning Source LLC
Chambersburg PA
CBHW050330120526
44592CB00014B/2130